T-rex Facts for Kids

Jacquelyn Elnor Johnson

www.CrimsonHillBooks.com

First edition, August 2022.

Cataloguing in Publication Data

Johnson, Jacquelyn Elnor

T-rex Facts for Kids

Description: Crimson Hill Books trade paperback edition | Nova Scotia, Canada

ISBN:	978-1-990887-14-7 (Paperback - Ingram)
BISAC:	JNF003050 Juvenile Nonfiction: Animals: Dinosaurs & Prehistoric Creatures JNF025150 Juvenile Nonfiction: History: Prehistoric JNF037050 Juvenile Nonfiction: Science & Nature: Fossils
THEMA:	RBX - Paleontology WNA - Dinosaurs & the Prehistoric World: General Interest YNNA - Children's - Teenage General Interest: Dinosaurs & Prehistoric World

Record available at https://www.bac-lac.gc.ca/eng/Pages/home.aspx

Book design: Jesse Johnson

Crimson Hill Books
(a division of)
Crimson Hill Products Inc.
Lawrencetown, Nova Scotia
Canada

Crimson Hill
Books

T-rex wasn't the biggest dinosaur that ever lived or even the largest meat-eating dinosaur. They were the apex predator, or top animal, everywhere they lived because they were fierce. They were also smarter than the plant-eating dinosaurs they hunted and ate.

T-rex is the most famous and popular dinosaur in the world.

How well do YOU know T-rex?

Tyrannosaurus rex [say this: Tie-ran-oh-sore-us wrecks] is the star of movies, books, video games, podcasts and TV specials.

You can often spot its big roaring face on tee shirts, mugs, and posters. Millions of T-rex toys and puzzles with toothy T-rex have been sold. There are T-rex masks, cartoons, coloring books, jokes and memes.

T-rex is a North American ancient animal that has millions of twenty-first century fans all around the world. That's amazing for an animal that's been extinct for almost 66 million years!

But who is this rock star dinosaur, really?

T-rex was big, bad and bold

Tyrannosaurus rex was one of the largest meat-eating land animals that has ever lived. And though no one has ever heard it, an animal that big and fierce-looking could probably make some noise. It could have been a really loud noise. Just like T-rex always does in the movies and on TV specials.

When you know all this about T-rex – big, mouth full of teeth, loud – you might think you already know just about everything about everyone's favorite dinosaur. But there are more strange and odd facts about Tyrannosaurus rex.

These are questions that have amazed and puzzled scientists for two hundred years or so, and new breakthrough discoveries happening today.

Slowly, T-rex is revealing some of its secrets! To find out what they are, and what truly amazing animals Tyrannosaurs were, you'll need to read this book!

What kind of animal were dinosaurs?

These are all the kinds of animals there are in the world today:

1. **Arthropods** [Arth-row-pods]. They're the insects, crabs and shrimp. Their hard shell skeleton is on the outside of their bodies.

2. **Fish**. They have a skeleton and gills and always live in water.

3. **Cnidaria** [Nie-dar-ee-a]. They are jellyfish and corals and always live in water. They have no skeleton.

4. **Amphibians**, like frogs and toads. They need to keep their skin wet, so live in water and near it. They are cold-blooded and have a skeleton.

5. **Annelids**, the worms. They are cold-blooded and have no skeleton.

6. **Reptiles**. They are snakes, lizards, turtles or birds. They all have a skeleton inside their bodies. Most of them are land animals, though some snakes and turtles also live in water.

7. **Mammals**. They are elephants, lions, whales, dogs, cats and many more animals, all with lungs and a skeleton. Humans are a mammal.

Scientists used to think T-rex was a sleek animal, like this model of a T-rex at a zoo. Now we know T-rex was big and burly, with a barrel-shaped belly.

Were dinosaurs reptiles?

Scientists think that dinosaurs were closest to modern reptiles. But dinosaurs aren't completely like any reptile alive today. For this reason, some scientists think dinosaurs might not have been reptiles, but were their own type of animal. If so, this is a type of animal that hasn't lived for millions of years.

Let's compare modern reptiles with what we know about dinosaurs, including T-rex. Then you can decide if you think T-rex was a reptile, or some other kind of animal.

All modern reptiles have scales. Almost all reptiles have babies born from eggs. Only a few types of snakes, all skinks and just one type of chameleon have their babies born alive. We think dinosaurs also had scales and some also had feathers. Dinosaur babies were born from eggs.

All reptiles have a backbone. They all have at least one lung. All the dinosaurs also had backbones and lungs.

All reptiles have a heart that pumps blood through their bodies. One dinosaur heart has been found and it is a lot like a modern bird's heart. Scientists are still searching for the answer to this question, "Did all dinosaurs have hearts?"

All reptiles today, except birds, are cold-blooded. This doesn't mean the blood in their body is cold. It means they have no way to control their own body temperature. To warm up, they need sun. To cool off, they need cool water or shade or burrows underground.

Dinosaurs couldn't have been cold-blooded and gotten as big as they did. They were probably like all modern birds who are warm-blooded.

Modern birds have hollow bones and also extra air sacs in their bodies. They also have feathers. Dinosaurs had hollow bones and extra air sacs in their bodies. Some dinosaurs, and maybe even some Tyrannosaurs like T-rex, might have had feathers.

So what <u>were</u> the dinosaurs, including Tyrannosaurus rex?

They couldn't have been an amphibian. All amphibians live in or very close to water. They all lay eggs in water.

T-rex couldn't be an arthropod. All arthropods have a hard shell. That's their skeleton. T-rex had a backbone and skeleton, like reptiles and mammals.

T-rex probably wasn't a mammal. It had scales and was far larger than any mammal of its time, or since then. Its body worked differently than mammals.

Most mammals have live babies and feed them mother's milk. Only five mammals alive today lay eggs. They are the duckbill platypus and four types of Echidnas [Uck-kid-nahs]. Echidnas are small animals. They only live in Australia or New Guinea.

T-rex couldn't be a cnidaria. They all live in the ocean.

So, what do you think the dinosaurs, including T-rex, really were?

Do you think T-rex was a reptile? Or maybe not? Scientists have been arguing about this for years! Someday, someone will finally answer this puzzling question of what all the dinosaurs, including Tyrannosaurus rex, really were.

T-rex Fun Fact:

Baby T-rexes had a small, thin skull and a long snout. They probably doubled in size in their first 6 weeks. As they got older, their skulls got a lot bigger, their snouts got shorter and their jaws got a lot stronger.

T-rex was a theropod

There were Tyrannosaurs on earth for 104 million years. T-rex, the largest, last and mightiest of the Tyrannosaurs, lived for only about 3 million years at the end of the Cretaceous Era.

The earliest Tyrannosaurs appeared on Earth 170 million years ago. They were smaller and faster but much less powerful than T-rex. The early Tyrannosaurs were a lot like very young T-rexes. That is small, quick and smart.

Here's what made all the members of the Tyrannosaurus family different than other dinosaurs. When they were adults, they had wide snouts, horn bones above and in front of their eyes and strange, joined-up nose bones. They also had two big bone ridges on their pelvises.

Tyrannosaurs lived in the Age of Dinosaurs. There were more types of dinosaurs in more shapes and sizes, eating many kinds of food and living everywhere on Earth. They lived during the Golden Age of Reptiles and also the Golden Age of Dinosaurs.

All the Tyrannosaurs were Theropods [theh-ruh-pods]. That's the group of meat-eating, or carnivore dinosaurs.

All Theropods had reptile hips. There were other types of dinosaurs that had bird hips, a different skeleton design. Strangely, all modern birds, who do have bird-hips, evolved from some of the smaller Theropods.

Theropods were the top hunter-predators during their time. They're also the most diverse looking group

Allosaurus

Carcharodontosaurus

Torvosaurus

Deinonychus

Velociraptor

Abelisaurus

Spinosaurus

Albertosaurus

Tarbosaurus

Theropod Dinosaurs

Tyrannosaurus Rex

Suchomimus

Giganotosaurus

Mapusaurus

Tyrannotitan

Carnotaurus

Acrocanthosaurus

Yangchuanosaurus

Coelophysis

among all the types of dinosaurs. A very small group of Theropods were omnivores. This means they ate both plants and meat.

Some other dinosaurs that were also Theropods are: Velociraptor, Spinosaurus, Oviraptor, Megalosaurus, Compsognathus, Carnotaurus and Allosaurus.

Types of Dinosaurs

Carnivore – They preyed on other animals because they only ate meat.

Herbivore – They only ate leaves, seeds, roots or fruits.

Omnivore – They ate plants and meat.

Sauropods [Sore-oh-pods] – They were the giant, long-necked plant eaters that walked on four legs. They all had lizard hips. All of them were extinct by the Cretaceous Era when T-rex lived.

Hadrosaurs [Had-row-sores] – They were the duck-billed dinosaurs and were herbivores.

Stegosaurs [Steg-oh-sores] – Slow-moving herbivores with bony plates or spikes on their backs.

Ankylosaurs [An-kill-oh-sores] – Herbivores with body armor.

Cerapods – Also called Ceratopsians, they were herbivores with horns and a bony neck frill.

Theropods – They were carnivores and walked on two legs.

Allosaurus was the top predator for millions of years, but then vanished. Paleontologists don't know why they died out. When this happened, T-rex became the top predator everywhere it lived.

Ornithopoda [Or-nith-oh-pod-a] – Bird-like dinosaurs that walked on two legs.

Pachycephalosauria [Pak-ee-seff-a-low-sore-ee-a] – Herbivores with thick, bony skulls that walked on two legs. They lived when T-rex did.

Non-avian dinosaurs – Every dinosaur except birds.

Saurischia [Sore-itch-ee-a] – All the dinosaurs whose hips were shaped the same as modern lizards.

Ornithischia [Or-nith-itch-ee-a] – All the dinosaurs whose hips were shaped the same as modern birds.

When did T-rex rule?

The first Tyrannosaurs appeared on Earth about 170 million years ago. For millions of years, they were a smaller dinosaur. They weren't the top animal. Other, bigger meat-eaters hunted them.

It was not until about 84 million years ago that Tyrannosaurs started to become bigger and stronger. By the late Cretaceous Era, in Laramidia [Lar-ah-mid-ee-a], Tyrannosaurus rex became the top predator. Other meat-eating dinosaurs were the top predators in other parts of the world.

T-rex ruled as Laramidia's top land predator from 68 million years ago to 65.5 million years ago.

Where did T-rex live?

T-rex was a Tyrannosaur that lived in Laramidia. That's the name for the ancient island that would eventually become part of North America. Other types of Tyrannosaurs lived before T-rex and there were other types of Tyrannosaurs that lived in Asia.

It could be that there were Tyrannosaurs in South America, or Africa, or elsewhere in the world, but they've never been found.

T-rex Fun Fact:
In times when there was less food, young Tyrannosaurs were able to slow down their growth so they needed less to eat.

Lythronax [Lith-row-nax], an early Tyrannosaur, is on display at the Natural History Museum of Utah.

Some early Tyrannosaurs walked across a land bridge to what is now Asia. It could be that Tyrannosaurs started in Asia, and some crossed a land bridge from there to what is now Alaska and moved south. That could have been long before T-rexes' time.

When T-rex was alive, Laramidia was a long island surrounded by ocean. Today, that's part of Western United States and Western Canada.

There may be Tyrannosaur fossils hidden in the rocks in Europe, South America, Africa or Australia still waiting to be discovered.

T-rex Fun Fact:

All the dinosaurs, including T-rex, died out after an asteroid hit Earth 65.5 million years ago.

Currently, there are nine types of Tyrannosaurs that have been discovered and named by scientists. It could be that there are many more waiting to be found. All the Tyrannosaurs lived near water. They never lived in deserts, because there wouldn't be enough food there for such large animals.

What was Laramidia like when T-rex was alive?

When they lived there, most of Laramidia was a tropical place. It was warm and humid, something like Florida is today in July and August. There was also more oxygen in the air. This climate helped trees and plants grow quickly. It helped many types of animals thrive.

With a lot of oxygen in the air, dinosaurs could get bigger as well as stronger. This climate would have been too hot and have too much oxygen for humans to survive, but it was ideal for reptiles, especially dinosaurs.

It was a lush, leafy semi-tropical world at the end of the Cretaceous Era. There were many types of plants and trees. The first flowers had appeared.

If you could visit, you would see all of the trees and plants that earlier dinosaurs knew, such as cycads, ginkgo and beech trees, grasses and ferns. Cycads are like palm trees. In the late Cretaceous there were also maple, ash, willow, and oak trees. There were flowering trees like magnolias and fruit trees like fig and breadfruit.

In this warm world, trees would have kept their leaves all year long. There would always be flowers and fruit.

T-rex Fun Fact:

Scientists haven't found dinosaur DNA, what we would need to recreate a dinosaur today, but there are some who say it might be possible to find dinosaur DNA, even though dinosaurs have been dead for so long. The oldest DNA scientists have recovered is from a tooth of a Wooly Mammoth that froze in the permafrost of East Siberia 1 million years ago.

A Harvard University scientist, geneticist George Church, is leading a project to recreate Wooly Mammoths. He has announced that the first calves could be born by 2028. If it's possible, this animal won't exactly be a Wooly Mammoth. It will be a Wooly-ized and supersized elephant that is able to survive the cold of Siberia. This is because you need a living host animal, like a normal elephant, to be able to use the DNA to create babies. Those babies would be one half Wooly and one half elephant. It could be a very odd animal!

Parasaurolophus

Amargasaurus

Styracosaurus

Pentaceratops

Pachycephalosaurus

Utahraptor

Olorotitan

Cretaceous
Dinosaurs

Diabloceratops

Carnotaurus

Tenontosaurus

Antarctosaurus

Kaprosuchus

Nanotyrannus

Velociraptor

Torosaurus

Tyrannosaurus Rex

Deinonychus

What other animals lived at the same time as T-rex?

The Cretaceous Era was the Age of Dinosaurs, and also the Age of Reptiles. T-rex was a very successful animal, living for millions of years, but there were many other dinosaurs, reptiles, amphibians, fish and insects that also thrived in this time.

One was Triceratops, a plant-eating dinosaur that T-rex hunted. Triceratops had horns on its face, a wide frill of bone to protect its neck and hundreds of teeth packed close together. These teeth worked like scissors, cutting up the tough leaves and tree branches it ate. Triceratops was a big, slow moving herd animal, something like modern bison.

Edmontosaurus was a duck-billed dinosaur and another animal that T-rex hunted.

How do we know about T-rex?

Everything we know about T-rex comes from what they left behind. That's their bones, teeth, eggs and trackways. All of these are usually fossils. Trackways are the footprints of animals that were walking or running.

Fossils are any part of an animal, or showing their behaviour, that has turned to stone.

T-rex had huge feet with three toes. When they were adults, their feet were 33 inches or 83 centimetres long and 28 inches or 71 centimetres wide. That's twice as big as a modern elephant's foot!

The fossil bones of a T-rex whose nickname is Sue.
Sue was discovered in 1990.

We know this from footprints they left and also from
their fossil skeletons. A skeleton is all the bones in an
animal's body. People also have skeletons.

What is a fossil?

When an animal dies, their bones slowly decompose
on or in the ground. This means they break down, rot
away and are gone. Very rarely, before this happens,
bones can turn into stone. This is called fossilization or
fossilisation.

Bones, teeth, claws, or eggs can be fossilized.

Here's how some parts of an animal can turn into

fossils.

1. **The animal dies.**

2. **The soft parts of the animal are eaten by other animals or they rot away,** leaving just the hard parts, like bones, spines, teeth, claws or horns.

3. **These hard body parts are covered** and buried by mud, sand, or silt.

4. **More sand or silt or mud lands on top of them.** This puts weight and pressure on the buried body.

5. **Water and minerals move into the bones or other hard body pieces,** gradually turning to stone. All of the real body parts are gone. Only the stone remains.

We don't really know exactly how long this whole process takes, but it could be millions of years. The reason most fossils that fossil-hunters find are from marine animals is because an animal that lives in water will sink to the bottom and could quickly be covered by silt or sand.

Land animals, like dinosaurs, did need to live close to water. Some of them would have died because they were caught in quicksand or buried by a mudslide. On land, usually scavengers scatter bones before they can be buried and, possibly, preserved as fossils.

Paleontologists are able to find some dino fossils because the Earth is always building itself up and tearing itself down at the same time. Rock layers are pushed up to the surface and mountains are created.

These layers are also always getting worn down by the weather and erosion. Wind, ice, rain, heat, and rivers cutting through mountains can cause fossils to move closer to the surface.

The other main reason fossils are found is just good luck. It might be that a sharp-eyed person spots something odd sticking out of the ground. They think it might be a horse skeleton, or maybe just a piece of wood.

They call the local university, or maybe the local heritage office and, sometimes, what they've found is something really remarkable, like a part of the jawbone or spine of a dinosaur!

Two types of fossils

Paleontologists look for body fossils and trace fossils.

- **Body fossils** are any part of a plant or animal. They could be leaves, bones, horns, quills, feathers or teeth.

- **Trace fossils** are evidence of an animal's behaviour. Some trace fossils are hand prints, foot prints, burrows, bite marks, eggs, nests or tail drag marks.

T-rex Fun Fact:
Paleontologists and dinosaur hunters have found only parts of 60 T-rexes and none of them is a complete animal. Sue, found in South Dakota in 1990, is the most complete T-rex ever found.

Why don't we find T-rex in permafrost?

Maybe you've read about recent discoveries of Wooley Mammoths being discovered in permafrost, in places like Yukon, Canada and Northern Asia. Permafrost is ground that is always frozen. It never melts in summer.

Wooley Mammoths lived millions of years after the dinosaurs vanished. Even though they're an ancient animal, when they're trapped in permafrost they aren't fossils. Their skin, hair and even their eyelashes are perfectly preserved.

Finding an ancient animal in permafrost is a bonanza for scientists. With skin, fur, and other soft tissues, there is much more information about the animal, and what it looked like, than just fossils could reveal.

There are no T-rex, or any other dinosaur, perfect remains frozen in permafrost because the world was warm when the dinosaurs lived. It was not an Ice Age. There was no polar ice at the North Pole, just open ocean.

Antarctica was further north back then, closer to South America and it was a semi-tropical place teeming with animals. In this warmer world, as in tropical places today, there is no frost in the ground to preserve some of the plants or animals that die.

T-rex Fun Fact:
T-rex had air vents in its head to cool its brain, the same as modern crocodiles have.

This is an artist's idea of what a young and furry T-rex might have looked like.

What did T-rex eat?

T-rex ruled for the last two million years of the Cretaceous Era in Laramidia. In this warm, wet world, there would have been plenty of other dinosaurs for T-rex to eat.

There also would have been some ferocious enemies. One was the giant crocodiles that lived both in the ocean and on land. Giant snakes, smaller reptiles and mammals that stole eggs from their nests and injuries from fighting were other dangers.

T-rex Fun Fact:
T-rex might have hunted alone or in packs.

Did T-rex have shaggy hair?

Most T-rexes probably didn't have hair. They lived where it was warm all year. This is because Laramidia was much further south than North America is today. Back then, Laramidia had the equator running through it. Places near the equator are always warm or hot.

But there was one T-rex that has been found in Alaska. It might have lived at a time when it was cooler there in winter. If so, it might have evolved to have a shaggy coat to stay warm. "Evolved" means changed, over time, to have a better chance to survive. All animals are constantly changing, or evolving, to adapt to where they live. This has always been true and is still true today.

Did T-rex have feathers?

Some dinosaurs had what scientists call protofeathers. This means something that will eventually evolve into feathers, but isn't really feathers yet. It's more like the stiff central barb of a feather. This barb might have some wisps on it. Velociraptor and Microraptor are two dinosaurs that we know had protofeathers.

Protofeathers can't do much. They aren't flight feathers. They aren't able to keep an animal warm. But they might have had bright colors that were useful for attracting a mate.

T-rex Fun Fact:
Dinosaurs thrived on Earth for more than 165 million years.

T-rex hunts along the shore among the cycad trees.

Protofeathers weren't a new dinosaur thing when T-rex was alive. There were Tyrannosaurs with protofeathers, but all of them lived long before T-rex's time.

Dilong [Dee-long], a small meat-eating dinosaur that lived in China, was covered in protofeathers. Dilong was a distant member of the Tyrannosaur family. It lived 65 million years before T-rex appeared on Earth. It weighed just 25 pounds, or 11 kilograms.

Another feathered Tyrannosaur relative called Yutyrannus [You-tie-ran-us] lived 125 million years ago in China. It was smaller than T-rex at about 30 feet or 9 metres long. Yutyrannus is the largest feathered meat-eating dinosaur yet discovered. Its feathers were up to 8 inches long. These feathers might have covered all of their bodies, like modern chickens.

Not very many T-rex fossils have been found, compared to some other types of dinosaurs. None of them had feathers. What fossil-hunters have found are fossils of T-rex skin. This is how we know that T-rex had scales on its neck, hips and tail.

It could be that baby or very young T-rexes did have feathers but lost them as they became juveniles. Juvenile for animals is the same as teenager is for humans.

What sounds did T-rex make?

It's fun to think about T-rex stomping around and roaring all the time. That's what they do in movies.

Real animals of today that roar, like lions, or bellow, like elephants or make any other loud noises don't make those noises very often, or hardly at all. T-rex was probably the same.

There are a lot of good reasons for an animal to be quiet. If you're a stealth hunter, you don't want your prey to know you're about to attack.

If you're worried about your enemies finding you and trying to eat you, you'd rather they didn't know where you are.

T-rex Fun Fact:
T-rex had 380 bones. Dogs have 321 bones. Adult humans have just 206 bones.

Here are the reasons animals DO make sounds:

1. To talk to each other, like when a baby wants to find her mother or one herd member wants to warn all the others of danger.

2. To attract a healthy mate.

3. To announce their own territory and warn other males to go find their own place to live.

4. To teach their babies, like when a male songbird teaches his song to his nestlings.

5. To scare off an attacker by sounding dangerous.

6. Or maybe just because they can.

T-rex might have roared, sometimes. Or maybe not. There are scientists who think it's possible, maybe even probable, that predator dinosaurs didn't roar. Instead, they say, there is evidence that what T-rex did is a low frequency booming sound.

Low frequency means very low bass sounds. Some are too low for humans to hear. Sounds that are too low for humans to hear are called "infrasounds." These sounds can travel long distances. They're like a private language for the animals that use them.

We know of several animals that are alive today that use infrasounds. Elephants use infrasounds to communicate with each other. So do pigeons. Tigers use infrasounds to drive away enemies.

There may be other animals that use infrasounds, including some ancient animals. Judging from the size and structure of their inner ears and their brains,

A hunting pack of T-rexes face a much smaller Ankylosaurus.

scientists strongly suspect that one of them was T-rex.

What could T-rex hear?

From the size and shape of the ear canal and their brain, scientists think that T-rex had very good hearing. This would help T-rex track their prey. T-rex could hear low-frequency sounds. If so, it would mean that the other animals T-rex hunted made those sounds.

What could T-rex smell?

A T-rex skull has large openings for their nostrils. That means nose holes. It also means that having a good sense of smell was something that was important for their survival, just as it is for modern animals like dogs, vultures and wolves.

T-rex had a sensitive snout. Some scientists say T-rex used this ability to measure the temperatures in their nests. They couldn't sit on their nests, so they probably used branches and leaves to protect and warm their eggs.

They'd also need a way to tell when their nests and eggs were getting too hot. This way was probably that they could sniff the temperature in their nests. If the nest got too hot, they could remove branches and leaves so air could cool the eggs.

Dinosaur mothers might even have taken their eggs in their mouths, when they were ready to hatch, and gently broken the shells. That's what modern crocodiles do.

What could T-rex see?

A T-rex eye was about as big as a grapefruit. That's large, but not nearly as big as the largest animal eye ever discovered. It belongs to a modern animal, the Colossal Squid. Their eye is as big as a soccer ball!

All animals that have eyes that point to the front are predator animals. That means hunters. Like all meat-eating dinosaurs, T-rex was a predator animal.

All predator animals have binocular vision. This means they're good at seeing things that are further away and all the way to the horizon. They need this skill to hunt.

T-rex's sharp binocular vision was one of the advantages that made it a powerful hunter and top predator.

Animals that have binocular vision also have good depth perception. Depth perception is being able to judge how far away something is.

The animals predators hunt for and eat could be other predators or they could be prey animals. Prey animals have their eyes on the sides of their heads. All the herbivore dinosaurs were prey animals.

Prey animals don't have good depth perception, so they aren't good at knowing how far away something is, but they're very good at seeing things that are close to them. Prey animals usually live in herds to protect each other.

T-rex Fun Fact:

All dinosaurs, including T-rex, constantly changed through their history. Some got smaller. Some got bigger. It all depended on the climate where they lived and how much food was available. This kind of changing is called evolving. The science of how Earth and everything alive on Earth is constantly changing is called "evolution."

Could T-rex taste their food?

Scientists study animals that are alive now to understand ancient animals. Modern carnivores don't have long, slow meals. They kill and eat their prey quickly, gulping it down. That's so they're sure to get full before some other animal tries to steal their dinner. They eat so fast, they probably don't really taste their food, or at least not the way humans can.

Animals need to be able to smell, and taste, when food has something bad in it that could make them sick, or it has gone rotten. All animals have the instinct to eat only healthy food and drink only clean, fresh water.

If a food smells OK and tastes OK, they eat it. Otherwise, even when they're really hungry or thirsty, they don't. This helps their species survive.

Dinosaurs survived for a very long time. They probably had the same instincts as modern animals do to only eat and drink food that is safe for them.

What made T-rex so dangerous?

Along with good eyesight and excellent hearing, T-rex had the advantage of being big as an adult. It had huge muscular jaws, teeth like knives, a powerful tail and short but strong arms.

Baby and juvenile T-rexes would grow up to have all these advantages, but were much less able to defend themselves or hunt for food. T-rexes probably lived in groups to protect their young.

Even T-rex was worried about the giant crocodiles that lurked in the water, just waiting to attack!

What colors was T-rex?

Modern animals use color as camo to hide from their enemies, or as bright colors to attract mates and possibly scare away enemies.

Did ancient animals, including T-rex, use color like modern animals do? Scientists have been asking this question for years. But when you only have fossils of footprints, bones, teeth and eggs, it's hard to know for sure what colors dinosaurs were.

Bodies break down as they become fossils. Melanin in skin or feathers is what gives them their colors. But melanin quickly breaks down and is gone. This is why scientists used to think that we'd never discover what colors dinosaurs were.

In this century, with breakthrough science and technology, ways have been found to reveal dinosaurs' true colors. New fossils are being found with some tissues and even feathers that are still there. With them, and breakthrough science, it might be possible to discover what colors all the dinosaurs were!

Using this new science, we now know that Microraptor, a small dinosaur with wings, had shiny black feathers all over its body, like modern crows and ravens.

Psittacosaurus [Sit-ta-co-sore-us], a large horned dinosaur with a parrot face that lived in Asia, was rusty red-brown. It was darker on its back than on its belly.

In the movies, T-rex is a dull brown, but that might be completely wrong. Scientists think T-rex was probably greens and browns, maybe with a camo pattern. There were horns above their eyes. T-rexes might have had a jaunty head crest, like Blue Jays do today.

Most modern animals tend to have one overall body color with brighter colors near their eyes. This color pattern is also true for humans. We have skin that's the same brownish or tanish color all over our bodies, but then usually have eyes and hair that's a dramatically different color. This works to draw attention to our faces. It also helps us recognize each other.

You could imagine a brownish, greenish and maybe dull camo T-rex, maybe with bright red on the bones above its eyes, or on its head or along the top of its

T-rex hunting a Hadrosaur.

back. With more T-rex fossils being found, and more breakthroughs in the lab, it could be that someday soon scientists will discover exactly what T-rex looked like!

T-rex Fun Fact:

Most Tyrannosaurs lived where it was warm and humid, but one called Nanuqsaurus [Na-nuk-sore-us] was a polar dinosaur that lived in what is now Alaska. Some scientists say it might have been covered in feathers or fur to keep warm.

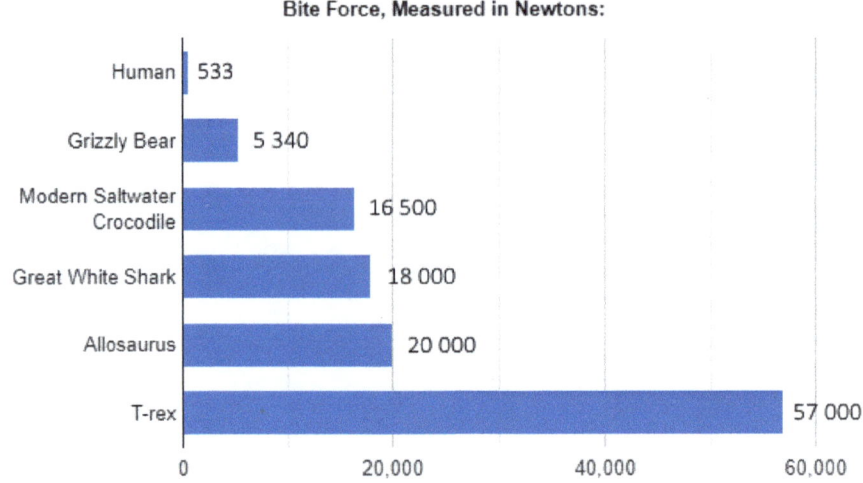

Bite Force, Measured in Newtons:

Human	533
Grizzly Bear	5 340
Modern Saltwater Crocodile	16 500
Great White Shark	18 000
Allosaurus	20 000
T-rex	57 000

CHOMP! T-rex bite force was FIERCE!

T-rex wasn't the biggest dinosaur that ever lived, but it did have the biggest dinosaur teeth ever found. It had a huge, powerful jaw filled with 60 curved teeth. Those teeth could be 12 inches, or 30 centimetres long. T-rex could chomp through bones and crush them.

Young T-rexes couldn't bite like the adults could. Babies and youngsters would need to eat small animals, reptiles or mammals and dinosaur eggs. They might also have eaten other baby T-rexes. Or they might have fed from the animals that adult T-rexes killed.

Adults had a more powerful bite than other meat-eating dinosaur. An adult T-rex bite was more powerful than any animal that has ever lived. It was up to 12,800 pounds of force per tooth. That's about the same amount of force there'd be if an elephant sat on you.

How do dinosaurs get their names?

Dinosaurs are usually named to honor where they are found or the people who found them.

This isn't true for Tyrannosaurus rex, whose name means, "The Tyrant Lizard King." T-rex wasn't named by Barnum Brown, the paleontologist who dug him up, but by another paleontologist who studied the fossils Mr. Brown and his team found.

In 1905, paleontologist Henry Fairfield Osborn was looking at those fossils in his lab. He thought they probably came from two different dinosaurs, but later changed his mind and said the fossils must be one animal. He named that animal Tyrannosaurus rex.

Just two years later, Mr. Brown found another T-rex, and this one was something rare, a nearly complete fossil skeleton.

Today, you can see the first named T-rex at Carnegie Museum of Natural History in Pennsylvania, United States.

Another famous paleontologist is John "Jack" Horner. He discovered that like many other animals, dinosaurs looked after their babies. He also said his research shows that many types of dinosaurs were social animals. This means they lived in groups.

The most famous paleontologist in Asia today is Xu Xing of China. Mr. Xu has found, described, and named 60 dinosaur species. All these dinosaurs lived in Asia. Some of them were Tyrannosaur cousins of T-rex.

What happened when?

BILLIONS of years ago:

4.6	Our solar system is formed.
3.7	The first one-cell animals appear.

MILLIONS of years ago:

530	The first fish appear in the ocean.
500	The first plants grow on land.
480	The first insects appear.
450	The first sharks evolve in the ocean.
385	Some fish leave the water to become amphibians.
330	Some amphibians evolve into the first reptiles.
230	A new kind of reptile is born – the dinosaurs.

170	**The first Tyrannosaurs evolve.**
130	The first flowers appear on trees and plants.
68	**Tyrannosaurus rex is the top predator in Laramidia.**
65.5	**The K-T Extinction ends the Age of Dinosaurs.**
2	The first humans appear in Africa.

THOUSANDS of years ago:

| 300 | Modern humans evolve in Africa. |

T-rex Fun Fact:

Fossil fuels like oil and gas aren't made out of animal fossils, so you aren't putting ground-up dinosaurs in your car's tank. The fossil fuels are coal, petroleum or oil, natural gas, oil shale, bitumen, tar sands and heavy oil. They all come from the remains of ancient plants. We use fossil fuels to heat and cool our homes, cook our food and power cars, trucks, busses and airplanes.

T-rex was large, but not the biggest meat-eating dinosaur that ever lived. That was Spinosaurus.

How big was T-rex?

T-rex adults could be 12 or 13 feet, or almost 4 metres tall. They could grow to be up to 13 metres long, or almost 43 feet. That's about as long as four alligators lined up snout-to-tail. An adult T-rex could weigh 7 tons or 6.3 tonnes, about the same as 93 adult humans.

A T-rex fossil skeleton named Scotty is the largest T-rex ever found. Scientists estimate that Scotty weighed almost 8 tons, or 7 tonnes. That would be 19,555 pounds, or 8,870 kilograms.

Scotty was 30 years old when he died, making him the T-rex that had the longest life that we know

Gigantosaurus, a meat-eating dinosaur, was bigger than T-rex.

about. Scotty is on display at Royal Saskatchewan Museum in Canada where you can visit him.

Tyrannosaurus rex was one of the largest meat-eating dinosaurs to ever live, but Spinosaurus [Spine-oh-sore-us] was the biggest. The next biggest dinosaur after Spinosaurus was Gigantosaurus [Gi-gant-oh-sore-us]. T-rex is in third place.

T-rex Fun Fact:
T-rex had three fingers on each hand. Two of these fingers had sharp curved claws that could be the size of bananas. Their claws were sharper than their teeth.

How fast could T-rex run?

"Trackway" is the name for a line of footprints showing where an animal walked or ran long ago. Trackways are fossil footprints. The actual footprint has turned to stone.

There are only a few T-rex footprints and trackways that have ever been found. Scientists use trackways to learn if animals were walking or running and how fast they were going. T-rex seems to have been like modern lions. It mostly walked and hardly ever ran.

When T-rex did run, it was probably for just a short distance. This is called a sprint. Though big and powerful, it would take a lot of energy for a T-rex to run, or even sprint! When they did, paleontologists and other scientists have figured out that T-rex was going about 18 miles per hour, or about 29 kilometres per hour. That's just a bit faster than a fit human can run.

One trackway shows that three T-rexes were walking together. They were going between 6.5 and 8.5 kilometres per hour, or 4 to 5.3 miles per hour.

That's walking, and only a bit faster than humans walk, but it's faster than most of the herbivore dinosaurs that T-rex hunted could walk. T-rex probably didn't have to run very often. Just walking was fast enough to catch dinner.

T-rex Fun Fact:

Of the millions of T-rexes that must have lived in their millions of years on Earth, only fossils from 25 animals have ever been found.

How smart was T-rex?

Scientists compare brain size to body size when they're trying to find out how smart an extinct animal was. Most dinosaurs didn't have very big brains. Like all animals, they were smart enough to find water, food and shelter and healthy mates, and defend themselves from enemies, but that's all they could do.

Tyrannosaurs could do all this and maybe more. The Tyrannosaurs, including T-rex, had brains that were twice as big, compared to their body sizes, as any other type of dinosaur. It was also an odd brain, compared to modern animals. It was long and tube-shaped. Scientists don't know why the shape was so odd, or what extra smart things their bigger brains helped T-rex do.

New research on birds suggests that brain size, compared to body size, might not give us the full story about how smart animals are. Songbirds have tiny heads with tiny brains inside them, yet some songbirds are able to do very smart things.

Birds' brains are wired to be extra efficient, using a different brain design than mammals, including humans, have. Since dinosaurs and birds are related, it could be that dinosaurs also had this brain design advantage.

How smart T-rex really was, and what it could do with a smart brain, are just two more of the fascinating questions scientist are striving to answer.

Why did T-rex have such tiny arms?

T-rex looks like a big, powerful animal with wimpy arms. So why would an animal that was the top predator everywhere it lived have short arms? Were they just to help it stand up after it had been resting or sleeping on the ground? Or did these little arms, only about 1 metre or 39 inches long, have any use at all?

Their arms were only about as long as an adult human's arms. T-rex's arms ended in hands with two real fingers and the stub of a third finger. The two fingers had long, sharp claws.

The arm bones show where muscles were attached. These muscles would have made their puny arms strong. So, scientists asked, why would T-rex need short but very strong arms? How did having puny arms help this animal survive?

And why did it need arms at all? Arms are easily broken. It takes energy to keep your arms working. It's better not to have them if you don't need them. If they had no use, in the millions of years T-rex existed, the arms would have vanished as the animal evolved.

That's exactly what happened with snakes' legs. They evolved from reptiles that did have legs. Snakes lost their legs to gain an important survival advantage. Legs use up energy and they take up space. Without legs, snakes could find shelter underground, in much smaller spaces. Without legs, their bodies needed less food to survive. They could move on their bellies. Legs weren't useful to them so they gradually shrank.

T-rex sends an Edmontosaurus family running for safety.

Today, the tiny nubs of leg bones are still visible on snakes' skeletons.

Could the same be true of T-rex arms? Were they shrinking away? If T-rex had lived for another million years or so, it would mean they'd still be here today. Would their arms have evolved to be almost nothing, like snakes' legs?

Scientists don't think so. They had many ideas about what these arms were for, but finally, only one answer fit with all the fossil evidence plus their knowledge of modern animals. The arms were short, but strong. They had sharp claws. They had to be for grabbing and holding onto struggling prey while T-rex slashed at the prey animal with their claws or bit and ripped at them with their terrifying teeth.

This Tyrannosaurus rex has made a mistake and gone too far into a swamp. That was the home of Tytanoboa [Tie-tan-oh-bow-a], the largest snake that has ever lived. Who do you think will win this ancient animal cage match?

What did T-rex eat?

Meat-eating dinosaurs needed to eat a lot to power their huge bodies. A T-rex adult would need to eat 200 pounds or 91 kilograms of meat a day to survive. That's about the same as a modern adult human who eats meat will eat in an entire year!

Like all modern cats, theropods like T-rex didn't eat anything except raw meat. T-rex teeth marks have been found on the fossil bones of other dinosaurs. They are plant-eaters like Triceratops, the club-tailed Ankylosaurus, the duck-billed Edmontosaurus and other Hadrosaurs. This is proof that T-rex ate all these dinosaurs.

T-rex the fighter!

Crunched up bones of other dinosaurs have been found in T-rex stomachs. Other dinosaur fossils have been found with T-rex tooth marks on their bones or pieces of T-rex tooth in their bodies.

There is a broken T-rex tooth stuck in a fossilized Hydrosaur's tail. Though it must have been badly wounded, there are signs the Hydrosaur lived because its tail wound had started to heal when it died.

T-rex Fun Fact:

T-rex teeth weren't sharp, but they were strong. Paleontologists call T-rex teeth "lethal bananas" because a T-rex bite would make their victims' bones explode!

T-rexes have been found with wounds probably made by other T-rexes, such as another T-rex fossil skeleton whose nickname is Stan. He had broken and healed ribs, a broken but healed neck, and a hole in the back of his scull that's the exact size as a T-rex tooth. That could have been what killed him.

T-rex could have been a stealth killer!

If T-rex had camo colors, it would be a sign that this animal was a stealth hunter. Like all cats today, they hide, sneak up on their prey, and then pounce!

This kind of hunting requires a bigger, better brain than the prey animal has. Stealth takes planning. It requires an animal to think through what could happen, and what they'll do about it.

T-rex might also have been a group hunter, or what scientists call a social animal. They live together and hunt together. Very young and juvenile T-rexes were long-legged, sleek, and fast runners. But they weren't very strong. Their teeth could easily break. Adult T-rexes were a lot larger, heavier, and slower. They could be stealth hunters but couldn't chase their prey.

But what if the young animals and the adults teamed up? What if they had a hunting plan? If that happened, then the younger T-rex family members could chase prey directly into the arms and jaws of their parents.

T-rex was smart enough to be a stealth hunter.

This is a sophisticated hunting strategy. It requires planning, cunning and communication between animals. It can be a very successful hunting strategy. Did T-rex know how to do this? And, if so, did they teach their children how to hunt this way? T-rex was a successful animal for millions of years. Like all animals, they must have evolved good ways to survive.

T-rex Fun Fact:

T-rex had a mouth full of serrated teeth. Serrated means like a steak knife. Their front teeth gripped their prey and pulled it apart. The side teeth tore the flesh of victims. The back teeth cut the meat into big chunks that T-rex swallowed. They didn't chew their food.

Was T-rex a hunter or scavenger?

Scientists used to think that all dinosaurs were slow-moving, heavy animals. Today, computer modeling is showing that the meat-eating dinosaurs like T-rex were big but they were faster, and probably smarter, than we used to think.

T-rex could run short distances at about 18 miles per hour, or 29 kilometres per hour. That isn't fast for an animal, but it is faster than a large modern animal, like an elephant, can run. It's also faster than humans can run.

So, T-rex had to be a hunter to survive. But was it also a scavenger, sometimes eating animals another animal had already killed?

The answer is probably yes. All animals are opportunity eaters. They eat what is easiest to get. If it is easiest to steal another animal's kill, they do. Many types of animals including reptiles and mammals do that today. T-rex probably did that millions of years ago.

T-rex enemies

Even though Tyrannosaurus rex was the apex, or top predator everywhere they lived, they still faced many dangers. The enemies of Tyrannosaurus rex that could injure or kill them include other big dinosaurs like Spinosaurus and Triceratops.

There were also illnesses that could make them very sick or kill them, such as avian flu and cancer. Animals

Triceratops was a plant-eater that T-rex hunted and ate.

that were very young, or old, or weakened by illness were easy prey for other carnivores.

Many dinosaurs probably died when their battle wounds got infected or broken bones meant they could no longer hunt, avoid predators, or find water. Others were probably killed in floods, landslides, forest fires started by lightning and in times when there wasn't enough rain, causing drought.

Why did T-rex have a tail?

T-rexes walked on their two back legs, but didn't stand up straight like kangaroos do. Instead, they leaned forward, using their large tails for balance. We know this because no fossils of T-rex trail drag marks have ever been found. This means they had to walk with their tails held above the ground.

Their tails were full of muscles. They might also have used their tails as a weapon, thrashing them at other animals.

Their tail might have helped T-rex be more nimble when it was fast-walking or running, allowing it to turn suddenly, like modern birds do when flying. The big muscles of their tails went to their thighs. This would have given them even more powerful legs.

T-rex babies

T-rex mothers built nests to shelter their eggs and babies. Their eggs were long and thin. No living animal has eggs like them.

We don't know if T-rexes were good parents. They might have cared for their young, like some birds do today. Or they might have had their eggs and abandoned their young, like modern turtles, but this seems less likely. T-rexes took a long time to grow up. They weren't very good at catching their own dinners when they were youngsters. They probably needed to live in a family group.

Very young T-rexes had a long skull, weak bones, small muscles, and thin teeth. They had small, sleek bodies. They could probably walk and run faster than adult T-rexes. They grew fairly slowly until they were 10 years old, then rapidly until they were about 18. As a juvenile, a T-rex would need to eat enough to gain 5

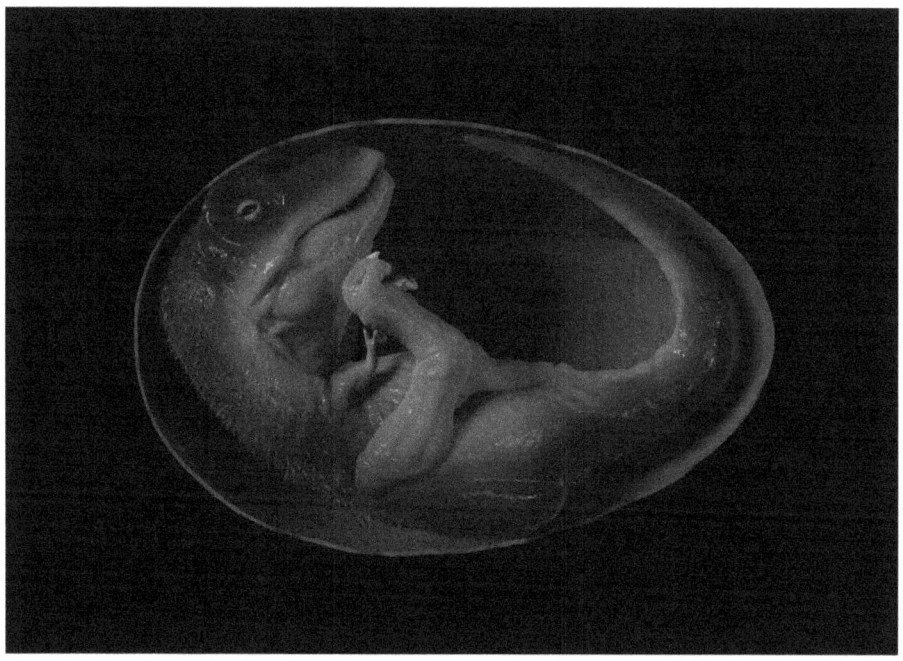

A T-rex inside its egg just before it's ready to hatch. Dinosaurs before they hatched looked surprisingly like the egg babies of modern birds.

pounds or 2.26 kilograms every day. That's 1,700 pounds or 760 kilograms a year!

We know how old fossil T-rexes were when they died because their bones form growth rings, one per year, just like trees do. You can slice through a T-rex fossil bone and count the growth lines to know how old that animal was when it died.

T-rex Fun Fact:

Tyrannosaurus rex was one of the last non-avian dinosaurs on Earth. Non-avian means "not a bird."

Other members of the T-rex family

Most Tyrannosaurs lived in Laramidia, what is now most of the Western half of Canada and United States. Some Tyrannosaurs that didn't live in Laramidia lived in Asia, mostly in what is now China and Mongolia.

T-rex only lived in Laramidia. No T-rex fossils have ever been found in Asia. Strangely, T-rex is a lot more like the Asian Tyrannosaurs than it is like the other Laramidia Tyrannosaurs.

Kileskus

Like all the early Tyrannosaurs, Kileskus [Kill-les-kus] was small. It weighed only about 100 pounds, or 40 kilograms. It lived 170 million years ago in Northern Asia.

Rajasaurus

Rajasaurus [Raj-a-sore-us] was an Asian Tyrannosaur that lived at the same time as T-rex. It lived in India.

At that time, the late Cretaceous Era, India was a large island off the East Coast of Africa. Later, India would travel north to crash into Asia, creating the Himalaya Mountains.

Guanlong

Guanlong [Gwon-long], whose name means "Crown Dragon," had long legs, a skinny body with a long tail,

Zhuchengtyrannus was discovered in China in 2010.

sharp teeth and three fingers on each arm. One finger had a long claw. It also had a crest on its head.

Guanlong lived in China.

Zhuchengtyrannus

Zhuchengtyrannus [Zoo-cheng-tie-ran-us] was found near the city of Zhucheng in China. It was almost as big as T-rex. It was found in a surprising place.

Only a few fossil bones of just one Zhuchengtyrannus were found when a construction company was digging the foundations for the new Zhucheng museum that would display other dinosaur fossils.

Construction stopped while the scientists recovered the fossils. Then the museum was completed. That's where the Zhuchengtyrannus fossils are now.

Chingkankousaurus

Chingkankousaurus [Ching-can-kow-sore-us] lived in China between 85 million years ago and 75 million years ago.

Very little is known about this Tyrannosaur because only one bone has ever been found.

Qianzhousaurus

Qianzhousaurus [Kee-an-zoe-uh-sore-us] was found in China in 2010 by Paleontologists Junchang Lu and Steve Brusatte. It was a small Tyrannosaur with a very long nose, so they gave it the nickname of Pinocchio rex.

Daspletosaurus

Fossils of this Tyrannosaur have been found in Alberta, Canada and Montana, United States. Daspletosaurus [Das-plet-tow-sore-us] preyed on Centrosaurus [Sen-tro-sore-us], a Ceratopsid, and Hypacrosaurus [Hi-pa-crow-sore-us], a Hadrosaur.

Compared to how big its body was, Daspletosaurus had the longest arms of any Tyrannosaur.

Back in 1996, when this U.S. stamp was issued, scientists didn't know that this animal, like all the Tyrannosaur family, would have had a bigger, rounder belly.

Could this Nanotyrannus have been a T-rex in disguise?

Alectrosaurus

Alectrosaurus [Al-leck-trow-sore-us] lived 96 million years ago in Asia. It wasn't much taller than an adult human is today.

Nanotyrannus

Some scientists suspect that Nanotyrannus [Nan-oh-tie-ran-us] wasn't another type of Tyrannosaur at all. Instead, they say, it was a juvenile, or teenage T-rex. This is because only the skull has been found, and it was of a young animal.

*This is Tarbosaurus, a Tyrannosaur cousin of T-rex.
Tarbosaurus lived in Mongolia, in Asia.*

Other scientists argue that Nanotyrannus can't really be a T-rex because it had more teeth than T-rex usually does. It was found in Montana.

Tarbosaurus

There are two things that are unusual about Tarbosaurus [Tar-bow-sore-us], compared to other Tyrannosaurs.

Thing one is Tarbosaurus could lock its lower jaw, though scientists don't know why this would be an advantage for this animal.

Thing two is many fossils of this dinosaur have been found, including full skeletons. Having a lot of fossils

These Bistahieversor twins have finding dinner on their minds!

to work with is a bonanza for scientists trying to understand Tyrannosaurs and all dinosaurs.

Tarbosaurus lived 70 million years ago in China.

Lythronas

Lythronas [Lie-throw-nacks] lived in Utah, United States, about 70 million years ago.

It is the earliest-known Tyrannosaur. Only part of a skull and skeleton from one Lythronas has ever been found.

Bistahieversor

Bistahieversor [Biss-ta-he-ver-sor] lived about 75 million years ago in South Laramidia where it is now land belonging to the Navaho people in New Mexico, United States.

It had 64 teeth. Another way it is different from other Tyrannosaurs is Bistahievesor had an opening above each eye. Scientists think this opening was for an air sac that would make their skull weigh less. This would make it easier for their neck muscles to hold their heads up.

Eotyrannus

Eotyrannus [EE-oh-tie-ran-us] was tiny, compared to T-rex. It was only about 15 feet, or 4.5 metres long and weighed about 200 to 500 pounds, or 227 kilograms.

It was an early Tyrannosaur and lived 170 million years ago. It was found on the Isle of Wight, an island south of England.

T-rex Fun Fact:

One reason T-rex might have had small arms is it needed thick neck muscles to support its head. Neck muscles and arm muscles both connect at the shoulder. It could be that the neck muscles took up so much space, there just wasn't enough left for larger arm muscles.

Alioramus might have looked like this.

Alioramus

Fossil remains from two Alioramus [Al-ee-oh-ray-mus] dinosaurs were found in Asia, but they appear to be from juveniles, not adults. This makes it difficult for scientists to describe what this animal was like. It lived 80 million years ago.

It had more teeth than other Tyrannosaurs and also had a row of five bony crests on the top of its snout.

T-rex Fun Fact:

Tyranno means tyrant in Greek. Saurus means lizard in Greek. Rex means king in Latin. So T-rex's full name in English is Tyrant Lizard King.

Prodeinodon

This is a named Tyrannosaur that might not ever have lived. Prodeinodon [Pro-dine-oh-don] was named for some dinosaur teeth found in China.

This dinosaur is in what scientists call a "wastebasket taxon" or "catch-all taxon." This means what scientists decide to call anything that doesn't seem to fit anywhere else until they can figure it out. Usually, it means they need to find more fossils to study.

Teratophoneus

Teratophoneus [Terra-tow-phone-ee-us] lived about 75 million years ago. Their name means "monster murderer" in Greek.

Only one group of Teratophoneuses has ever been found in what is now Utah, United States. They were four, or maybe five animals. The youngest was 4 years old and the oldest was an adult who was 22 years old. They all died at the same time, possibly swept away by a flood or in a landslide.

Albertosaurus

Albertosaurus [Al-bert-oh-sore-us] was about half as big as T-rex. It's named for the province in Canada where it was found.

As a juvenile, it needed to eat enough meat to gain 250 pounds or 113 kilograms per year.

Twenty-six Albertosaurs were found together in a bonebed in Alberta. The oldest was 24 years old and the youngest was a two-year-old. They were probably hunting as a pack.

Nanuqsaurus

Nanuqsaurus [Na-nuk-sore-us] lived in what is now northern Alaska about 69 million years ago. Its name means "polar bear lizard."

Only part of a skull and some teeth from one animal have ever been found, so we don't know much about this animal. It might have had feathers to keep warm in the darker, cooler months.

We DO know that there was no polar ice cap at that time. There would have been a temperate forest climate in Alaska in the Cretaceous Era.

However, as is true today, there would still have been a long, dark winter. Scientists believe the trees of that time must have evolved a way to go dormant during the darker months.

But what did the animals do? How did they find enough to eat in the months when the trees were sleeping? Did they migrate south like many birds do today? Did they hibernate, like modern animals in cold parts of the world do?

No one knows yet, but someday, scientists may find the answer.

Are there more Tyrannosaurs?

The Tyrannosaurs in this book are the ones scientists have found, described and named so far. Over their millions of years living almost everywhere on Earth, scientists think that many more Tyrannosaurs probably evolved to suit the climate when and where they lived. This means there are probably many more dinosaurs, still hidden in ancient rocks, just waiting to be discovered!

The story of the forgotten T-rexes

The very first T-rex fossils discovered were teeth, found by Joseph Liedy in 1856 in Western Canada. The first almost complete T-rex skulls and part of the skeletons of many T-rexes were found about 20 years later in Alberta, when T-rex got its first name, Manospondylus gigas [Man-oh-spawn-dill-us gee-gas].

These fossils sat forgotten for more than a century. Finally, someone gave them another look in the early 2000s and made a HUGE discovery. These long-overlooked skulls and bones weren't the mysterious Manospondylus gigas. In fact, they belonged to several 'lost' T-rexes!

T-rex Fun Fact:

In 2020, the fossil skeleton of a T-rex nicknamed Stan was sold at an auction to a private collector. That buyer paid $31,800,000 American dollars for Stan.

The skies darkened and rained burning stones on the last day of the dinosaurs.

Why is T-rex extinct?

There might still be dinosaurs today, perhaps even Tyrannosaurus rex, except for a freak accident that happened millions of years ago and light years away from Earth, far out in Space. One asteroid happened to bump into another. It happens all the time, but this time was different.

One travelling piece of rock hit another, knocking it just a little bit out of its orbit. That tiny change sent this space rock, or asteroid, on a collision course with Earth. This asteroid was travelling 67,000 miles per hour, or 108,000 kilometres per hour. It slammed into

Earth just off the coast of what is now Yucatan, Mexico.

It could be that a few dinosaurs happened to glance up and see a fireball moving across the sky as it grew larger. Perhaps they even wondered what it could be, before going back to having their ordinary day.

And then the asteroid hit Earth. Every living thing that was close to this impact site would immediately have been vaporized. Further away, there would have been shock waves everywhere on Earth as these waves travelled through Earth's core.

These shock waves would have caused earthquakes, volcanos, and tsunamis. Tsunamis are massive ocean waves that wash up on shore, causing death and destruction.

All of this would have killed many plants and animals, including many dinosaurs, within just minutes of the time the asteroid struck Earth. For those left alive, what came next was even worse. The skies filled with ash and smoke, blocking out the sun. Fire-hot stones rained down on any animal that couldn't find shelter.

T-rex Fun Fact:
Like modern birds, Tyrannosaurus rex had bones that were almost hollow. Hollow bones are strong but weigh less. This would have helped T-rex be strong and also able to move faster and be more agile.

T-rex never lived in and terrorized a city, except at the movies!

At first, those dinosaurs that survived the asteroid hit might have lived off eating all the plants and animals that didn't. Soon, most of the grasses and trees also died. Their seeds would lay dormant in the ground until clean air, sunshine and the rains returned.

We don't know how long it took for Earth to heal itself after this disaster. It might have been months, or years, or even hundreds of years. Of every four species that lived before the asteroid hit, three died out after the asteroid hit Earth. That probably included most, and maybe all, the dinosaurs.

Tyrannosaurus rex lived for almost 20 million years and then, suddenly, they were gone. The asteroid hit caused a mass extinction on Earth that scientists now call the K-T Extinction Event. It is the biggest global disaster we know of, and it happened 65.5 million years ago.

While many plants and animals were gone forever, Earth would recover. Small animals that lived in burrows or could hide deep in rocks or caves or cold water and could still find something to eat survived. They would become the ancestors of the new life that would rise up to take the place of all the animals that had vanished.

Could T-rex return?

In movies, T-rex returns to a world that is very different than it was when T-rex ruled. But could a real-life T-rex return?

Right now, there are scientists who say it could happen. One of them is paleontologist John "Jack" Horner. He is a famous paleontologist who was a consultant for the Jurassic Park movies. Mr. Horner is searching for dinosaur DNA. If he can find it, he thinks it could be possible to make a new animal that is something like a dinosaur.

It's a very complicated task, but it might be possible. The result wouldn't be a T-rex as it used to be. That's because it would be necessary to take T-rex DNA and introduce it into an animal that is as close to T-rex as possible. That animal, alive today, is a chicken.

The babies of a chicken with dino DNA wouldn't be true dinosaurs. They'd be dinosaurized chickens. That's a creature that has never existed and wouldn't exist, except if it becomes possible to create it in a laboratory.

There are many challenges to overcome before this can happen, but it might, in your lifetime!

Should dinosaurs return to Earth?

This isn't an easy question to answer. It would be fascinating to be able to discover what dinosaurs really looked like and how they lived their lives. If they came back, we would be able to finally answer the many questions there are about them.

But T-rexes couldn't live for long in today's climate, where there is less oxygen in the air, less territory for large animals in tropical places and no large herbivores for them to eat. They couldn't survive in our world, just as we couldn't survive in their world.

In the future, it might be possible to build a tropical park with a huge dome roof and fill it with high-oxygen air. This might be something like The Eden Project in England. It's a vast roofed tropical garden in Cornwall. This leads to some interesting questions:

1. If The Eden Project was hundreds of times bigger, would that be enough space to create a wild world for T-rex and other 21st century dinosaurs? How would we feed them? We wouldn't want them eating each other.

2. How would we pay all the money it would take to give them their ideal dino-world climate and keep them healthy?

3. Where would we put them? They'd need a big space to be wild. It wouldn't be fair to put them in a small space, like at a zoo.

4. Every animal has their place in their world. What modern animal would we destroy to make a place in nature for dinosaurs? It would need to be a large animal that lives in warm places. So, would that be elephants? Bison? Who could we do without, to get the dinosaurs back?

Scientists say we need a good reason to bring dinosaurs back to earth, if we can figure out how to do this and decide to do it. Curiosity about these animals is one reason, but is it a good enough reason? Should we do something just to get to say that we did it?

What do you think?

Museum dinos

Sue the T-rex is on display at the Field Museum of Natural History in downtown Chicago. She's the most complete T-rex that has ever been found. That was in 1990, in the Hell Creek Formation in Montana. Sue's skull is 5 feet, or 1.5 metres long.

Sue the T-rex might be a female dinosaur, or maybe not. Scientists aren't sure yet. She got her name because the dinosaur hunter who found her is paleontologist Sue Hendrickson.

Before Sue was found, scientists thought that T-rex was a large but sleek animal. Sue had belly bones below her ribs. Sue proves that T-rexes had more of a

Sue the T-rex now lives at the Field Museum of Natural History in Chicago where you can visit her.

heavy barrel shape. Sue the T-rex also shows how finding the remains of just one animal can change what we know and understand about dinosaurs.

T-rex ruled for more than 2 million years. They were magnificent, amazing, and very successful animals, for a very long time.

Some paleontologists believe that when the K-T Extinction Event happened, all the dinosaurs including T-rex were already in decline. Their best days had come and gone.

The Age of Reptiles was coming to a close. This might be true.

We have learned so much about them, but there are still many questions for scientists to answer about The Age of Dinosaurs. It's thrilling to wonder about them and their real lives and imagine what it must have been like, when T-rex ruled Laramidia!

Thanks for reading!

Jacquelyn

T-rex Fun Fact:

The only modern animals that roar are mammals. T-rex is more closely related to alligators and birds. They make their sounds with their mouths closed. T-rex probably didn't roar. It is more likely that T-rex rumbled, like elephants do today.

T-rex Fun Fact:

Tyrannosaurs didn't become adult animals until they were 18 years old. The oldest T-rex found died when he was 30, leading paleontologists to believe that they only lived until they were around 30 years old.

About the Author

Jacquelyn Elnor Johnson started telling stories to entertain her younger sisters when she was 10. They were a tough audience! By age 15, she was a writing for the local newspaper and had written her first book. She went on to have careers in writing for and editing newspapers and magazines and teaching journalism in United States and Canada.

In 2014, she moved with her family to Nova Scotia, drawn by the opportunity to live near the ocean. A life-long pet lover, she is the bestselling author of 13 books about caring for and enjoying pets and animals, including **I Want A Bearded Dragon** and **The Complete Bearded Dragon Care Book**.

She also writes novels including the Morley Stories series for girls ages 10 to 13.

Find all her books and more at
www.CrimsonHillBooks.com

PHOTO CREDITS

Our sincere thank you to these talented artists:

Lead artist **Daniel Eskridge**, and:

Shutterstock: **Milena Sabeva, Catmando, Hershel Hoffmeyer, Esteban De Armas, Lothar Dieterich, Ferhat Cinar, Elenarts, Michael Rosskothen, Catwalker and David Roland.**

Pixabay: **Katie Swarm, Willgard Krause, Lauren Buckels, DangrafArt, F. Muhammed and Pete Linforth**.

And thank you to the Natural History Museum of Utah and the Field Museum of Natural History in Chicago.

LOVED all these T-Rex facts?

Discover MORE with these great reads from Crimson Hill Books:

- **Fun Dog Facts for Kids**
- **Fun Cat Facts for Kids**
- **Fun Leopard Gecko and Bearded Dragon Facts for Kids**
- **Fun Reptile Facts for Kids; Lizards, Turtles, Crocodilians, Snakes and Birds**
- **Fun Pony Facts for Kids**
- **Fun Horse Facts for Kids**
- **Fun Bird Facts for Kids**
- **Fun Backyard Bird Facts for Kids**
- **Fun Insect Facts for Kids**

And Don't Miss:

- **Dinosaur Facts for Kids**
- **T-rex Facts for Kids**

www.ingramcontent.com/pod-product-compliance
Lightning Source LLC
Chambersburg PA
CBHW051551120626
46551CB00013B/1466